Presented By

Dr. Jody Sims

LOCAL AUTHOR

2013

Soul Provider

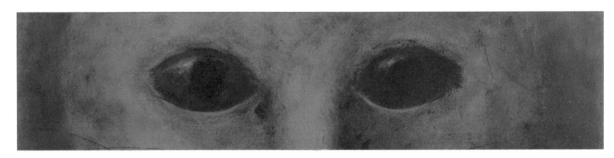

CONVERSATIONS WITH MY CAT

A Survivor's Journal

ISBN-10:0-9897892-0-9

ISBN-13:978-0-9897892-0-2

*"When you stand
and share your story
in an empowering way,
your story will heal you
and your story will
heal somebody else."*

– Iyanla Vanzant

What Happened . . .

I couldn't remember the last time I laughed. Everything made me cry. I was hiding out, waiting for these feelings of doom to pass . . . trying to pretend that everything would be ok . . . waiting for life to get back to normal. Unfortunately, normal never happened. Life just kept getting more and more complicated and less and less fun.

Two years prior I was working as the Chief Advancement Officer for a large non-profit organization. It was a demanding job, but even more so when I was put in charge of its 100th Anniversary. Long days, evenings and weekends were the norm.

Three days before one of those anniversary events, I received a phone call from the hospital trauma unit, telling me my partner Susanne had been rear-ended by a semi-trailer truck. She suffered a brain injury, a mangled leg, and many other complications which left her unable to work, drive, read a book or remember things from one minute to the next. Over the next seven months, I organized drivers, doctor appointments and social connections for her, then sped off to work.

Then came another test of my strength . . . I found a lump under my arm.

What Happened . . .

For days I didn't tell anyone. How could I tell Susanne? How could I tell my boss? This had to be the worst timing in the world.

When I finally got the courage to go to the doctor, I was diagnosed with stage three breast cancer. After second and third opinions from both western and eastern medical professionals, I chose my course of treatment: I would participate in the iSPY2 clinical trial for 12 weeks, followed by standard-of-care chemotherapy for 12 weeks, then surgery, and finally 32 days of radiation. During this time, I would also consult with a medical intuit and receive energy chiropractic.

It all happened so fast. I never cried.

Fast forward one year later . . .

I was done with chemo and surgery and was just about halfway through radiation therapy when, ironically, the hardest part of this journey began.

I may have missed this from the cancer class, (yes there are cancer classes, and I failed to attend any of them) but turns out cancer can be fatal. Really? This hit me like a brick . . . now. Of course I know people die from cancer, but not for one second did I think I would. I never went there. Instead, I just put my head down, did what I needed to do and endured the assault on my body.

What Happened...

I approached my cancer just like a work project – got organized, gathered my team, strategized, and implemented a plan.

I thought I was doing ok, but then . . .

My beloved Aunt Pauline passed away. My dear friend passed a week later. And then my boss came to tell me I would not have a job to go back to.

The financial drain was enormous, the emotional stress was devastating. Grieving, exhausted, hurt, enraged, and paralyzed with fear, I felt myself slipping into a very dark place.

I can't really explain what happened next, other than to say I allowed my instincts to take over. I began searching online for an art class!

This description of abstract art really caught my eye:

ABSTRACT ART: a visual language of form, color and line to create a composition which may exist with a degree of independence from visual references in the world.

What Happened . . .

I had no experience with abstract art, but this definition seemed
to perfectly describe how I felt about myself. In my mind, I was
an abstract of my former self – both physically and emotionally.

Then I found a class. It met once a week on Monday afternoons.
I had immense fatigue at this point so anything more would not
have worked. It was taught by Reed Cardwell, whose own art felt
amazingly tragic, intense, filled with despair and wonderful to me.
I knew I wanted to be in his class!

I walked into the first day of class and was greeted by four women
and two men. They welcomed me with big smiles and happy faces.
I set out my paints and put my crisp new canvas on the easel, then
waited for instruction.

Reed announced that class was in session. He then reminded everyone
that he does not assign anything. He also explained that he doesn't
teach technique. Then he looked at me and asked if I had something
in mind to paint – everyone is expected to be ready to paint!

To say I was panicked was an understatement. It had been years
since I painted anything. I had no ideas. I had no technique! How in
the world could I have made such a huge mistake?!?

So I answered . . ."Yes, I have something to paint."

What Happened . . .

I picked up a brush and dipped it into black paint, took a deep breath, then sketched the outline of a cat. It was nothing more than a cartoon. Hoping no one was watching, I added some color.

Then something really special happened . . .

Reed took a seat next to me. He explained "Abstract art is very broad. You know that's a cat. I know that's a cat. But we both know it's not really a cat. It's abstract."

Aha! I was right where I needed to be. I knew I could do this!

It was Reed's suggestion that I paint a series of something so I could see my progress. The cat face (an outline of my real life cat) was the only idea I could come up with. It wasn't planned, but by using the same image for every painting, I felt free to release my feelings without having to think about "what" to paint or its position on the canvas. I could be totally in the moment and in the flow.

Still unable to directly ask for help or tell anyone how I was feeling, I began a conversation with myself through these paintings. The homophones served as a kind of secret code into my thoughts and needs. Upon completing each painting, I wept.

The rest of the story follows . . .

HOMOPHONE: a word that is pronounced the same as another word but differs in meaning.

What

A better title might be "WTF?@#!"
The first time I really "heard" my diagnosis was after I completed all the chemo and surgery and just before radiation therapy was about to begin. The doctor told me I would not be able to work for at least 3 more months. This got my attention!
He used the words life threatening and aggressive cancer. What?
It hit me like a jolt of electricity reverberating to the bone.
How did I not hear this before?

"You haven't seen a tree until you've seen its shadow from the sky."
                                                            – Amelia Earhart

Black and Blue

Battered and bruised, exhausted and grief-stricken.
That pretty much described me near the end of radiation
treatments when overwhelming fatigue set in.
Feeling disoriented.

"We are all in this together – by ourselves." – Lily Tomlin

Where

Where am I?
Where am I going?
Where is my life?
Where can I hide?
Where are the clowns?
Where?

"How often I found where I should be going only by setting out for somewhere else."

– Buckminster Fuller

Blew on Blue

The song by Bobby Vinton, *"blue on blue, heartache on heartache . . ."* kept playing in my head. It was a feeling of sinking into sadness and grief as more and more crap kept piling on.

"Blue, here is a shell for you. Inside you'll hear a sigh, a foggy lullaby."

– Joni Mitchell

Eye See Red

I had been fighting off death for a year and now life was picking a fight with me! Rage. Hurt. Betrayal. Injustice. FEAR.

"I've learned that people will forget what you said, people will forget what you did, but people will never forget how you made them feel."

– Maya Angelou

When

When will these feelings of anger, sorrow and despair go away?
When will there be good news?
When will life be normal again?
"When" is an attempt to tap into my inner Buddha – where there
is no time or space – hopefully rendering these questions irrelevant.

"Life is eternal. You have plenty of time." – Louise Hay

Something I Red

I could no longer enjoy my morning routine of sipping on a cup of coffee, kitty in my lap, reading the newspaper. It felt like there was nothing but bad news.
I had no ability to compartmentalize it or detach from it.
I was hyper-sensitive to everything I read.
I had to stop reading the newspaper.

"Follow your instincts, that's where true wisdom manifests itself."
– Oprah Winfrey

Here to Hear

I painted *Here to Hear* on a larger canvas.

Perhaps this message needed to be big and loud in order for me to hear it.

It was telling me to stop and LISTEN.

Hear the birds singing outside the window.

Hear my lover whisper in my ear that she loves me.

Hear my cat purring as he nestles his warm body next to my heart.

Quiet my mind.

Hear life.

Listen!

"Divine love always has met and always will meet every human need."

– Mary Baker Eddy

Rays Me Up

This one started out to be "isle have another" with colors like
a tequila sunrise. It reflected how I wanted to feel – uplifted and high.
I changed the message to "rays me up" because I realized I needed
more than a temporary fix.

*"Without leaps of imagination, or dreaming, we lose the excitement
of possibilities. Dreaming, afterall, is a form of planning."*

– Gloria Steinem

How Grate Thou Art

I began to question the wisdom of spending so much time
painting this silly cat face over and over. I was filled with doubt.
Was I going crazy? Was this art?
Then I lined up all the completed canvases in order.
For the first time, I realized I wasn't just painting a cat face.
I was having a conversation with myself.
I no longer cared whether or not this was art or if I was going crazy.
I started to feel the healing.
I found the strength to continue.

"My own strength is the best strength I can have." – Annie Lennox

Prey For Me

Something dramatically changed when I completed *Prey for Me*.
There was an energy shift the minute I painted these words onto
the canvas. I found myself chanting "pray for me" over and over
in my mind.
It turned out to be my cry for help.
It was radically life changing.

*"Courage does not always roar. Sometimes courage is the quiet voice
at the end of the day saying, I will try again tomorrow."*

– Mary Anne Radmacher

The Other Sighed

I believed this to be my positive affirmation that there was another side to my upset life. Perhaps if I repeated this over and over like a mantra . . . took deep breaths . . . released many sighs . . . maybe I would eventually get there.

"Every moment wasted looking back, keeps us from moving forward."

– Hilary Clinton

End of Daze

Although it may seem dark and haunting, it actually was a
breakthrough moment for me to paint *End of Daze*. For the first time,
my cat's eyes were not looking back at me as if waiting
for an answer. Somehow I knew that my future cat paintings
would not have deer-in-the-headlight expressions.
I no longer felt dazed.

*"Let yourself be drawn by the strange pull of what you love.
It will not lead you astray."* – Rumi

Soul Provider

Soul Provider is the climax of my journey back to life. I had been
desperately searching for myself. When I looked in the mirror,
I saw a stranger. When I moved my body, everything hurt.
When I tried to speak, I could only cry.
As I completed this painting I was washed over by a knowing
that I was the sole provider of myself. Only I could save me.
I must have the power to do it. This was life or death.

*"We are not held back by the love we didn't receive in the past, but
by the love we're not extending in the present."*

– Marianne Williamson

A Knew Day

What I know for sure:

1. Every day is a new day and a chance to begin again.
2. Life changes in a moment.

Oddly, this is very grounding.

"Nobody can go back and start a new beginning, but anyone can start today and make a new ending."

– Maria Robinson

Past Do

A personal philosophy I shared so adamantly with others,
had now become vividly meaningful to me.
"It matters not what you did or didn't do in the past.
It only matters what you do from this day forward."
The present is my past. DO something.

*"Her heart felt not so much broken as just ... empty. It felt like she was
an outline empty in the middle. The outline cried senselessly for the
absent middle. The past cried for the present that was nothing."*

– Ann Brashares

Our of Need

Physically, emotionally, and now financially drained.
I had to let go of pride and admit that my resources
were tapped. I could no longer provide for my family.
Asking for help was one thing . . . opening my hands
and heart to receive was more humbling than
I could ever have imagined.

"Go to your fields and your gardens, and you shall learn
that it is the pleasure of the bee to gather honey of the flower,
But it is also the pleasure of the flower to yield its honey to the bee.
For to the bee a flower is a fountain of life,
And to the flower a bee is a messenger of love,
And to both, bee and flower, the giving and the receiving
of pleasure is a need and an ecstasy."

– Kahlil Gibran

Leased Resistance

All my life I've been told that taking the path of least resistance
is a bad thing – the easy way out.
It's clear to me now that it is NOT!
Resistance causes pain.
Why intentionally go down a path that causes pain?
To heal from life's challenges, to embrace a new day,
to begin again . . . I must follow my heart.
If I follow my heart, I will find my path of least resistance.
The pain will go away . . . I will feel joyful.

*"This is your time and it feels normal to you, but really, there is no normal.
There's only change and resistance to it and then more change."*

– Meryl Streep

Know Greater Love

We walked through the fire together.
My partner, lover, best friend . . .
a daily inspiration of what love is.
Gentle.
Peaceful.
Emotional.
Individual.
Evolving.

"He found me when my mind and soul were hungry and thirsty, and he fed them till our last hour together. It is such comradeships, made of seeing and dreaming, and thinking and laughing together, that make one feel that for those who have shared them there can be no parting."

– Edith Wharton

Sees the Day

I have a cartoon on my desktop of a woman standing in front of a
building reading a sign that says "Seeking Enlightenment, Inquire Within."
It shows her looking for the door, but there is no door.
The continuing journey to understanding my place in the universe and the
challenges I face along the way are unique, personal and often confusing.
But those wonderfully insightful moments, like when I realized there
was no door . . . that I AM the door . . . Wow!
Maybe I'll paint dogs!

"You gain strength, courage and confidence by every experience in which
you really stop to look fear in the face. You are able to say to yourself,
'I have lived through this horror. I can take the next thing that comes along.'
You must do the thing you think you cannot do."

– Eleanor Roosevelt

*"Could fulfillment ever
be felt as deeply as loss?"*

– Kiran Desai

Acknowledgments

Many thanks and much gratitude to:

Susanne for being by my side every step of the way – nourishing
my body, mind and soul.

Scout and Beau for your daily reminders of how to live in the moment.

My infusion team – Eric and Barb – for your positive and healing energy
on so many long days. Your gift of time was epic.

Ellen for teaching Susanne the Brazilian toe technique.

Ann and Gabe for organizing Chef Rosie's meal deliveries and to all
who contributed to this service – friends, family and people I've yet to meet.

Jennifer for the midnight ride to the hospital.

Art teacher Reed Cardwell and my classmates at the Art Academy – Kathy,
Pat, Kanti, Fani, Mike and Bill – for your contagious passion to become
better artists and for sharing your abstract view of the world.

Krista, Nora and Mom – my cousin, aunt and mother – fellow survivors who
read an early draft of the book and responded with so much enthusiasm.

Sepi for your great timing.

Mary Ellen for recognizing a need and organizing an unprecedented
effort to help – along with Paula, Cindy, Liz and Eric.

Mary and Marcia for the gift of a much-needed vacation.

My Facebook friends, who by "liking" my paintings as I posted them,
gave me the confidence I needed to forge ahead.

Family and friends for your generosity – taking me to a new level of understanding
the beautiful and humbling lesson of giving and receiving.

A ride here, a ride there, a walk in the park, a visit, a text message,
a phone call, an inspirational book, a cozy cap, thoughtful greeting cards
from so many people . . . I could never list you all here. I'm so grateful
for your friendship and caring and buoyed by your acts of love.

xo

© 2013 SUSANNE WHITING.

Jody lives in San Diego, CA with her partner
Susanne and their cats – Scout and Beau.
For more information visit **www.jodysims.com**

CPSIA information can be obtained
at www.ICGtesting.com
Printed in the USA
LVIW02n0015120913
351955LV00001B

9780989789202